quilt remix

Spin Traditional Favorites into 10 Fresh Projects

EMILY CIER

Text copyright © 2010 by Emily Cier

Artwork copyright © 2010 by C&T Publishing, Inc., and Emily Cier

Publisher: Amy Marson

Creative Director: Gailen Runge

Acquisitions Editor: Susanne Woods

Editor: Liz Aneloski

Technical Editors: Sandy Peterson and Gailen Runge

Copyeditor/Proofreader: Wordfirm Inc.

Cover Designer: Kristen Yenche

Book Designer: Amy Gonzalez Daniel

Production Coordinator: Zinnia Heinzmann

Production Editor: Alice Mace Nakanishi

Illustrator: Emily Cier

Photography by Christina Carty-Francis and Diane Pedersen of C&T Publishing, Inc., unless otherwise noted

Published by C&T Publishing, Inc., P.O. Box 1456, Lafayette, CA 94549

Library of Congress Cataloging-in-Publication Data

Cier, Emily.

Quilt remix : spin traditional favorites into 10 fresh projects / by Emily Cier.

    p. cm.

ISBN 978-1-57120-960-3 (softcover)

1. Patchwork--Patterns. 2. Quilting--Patterns. I. Title.

TT835.C4985 2010

746.46'041--dc22

                    2010007571

Printed in China

10 9 8 7 6 5 4 3 2 1

acknowledgments

Sean … for being there for me through every step of the way. He is truly the most quilt-literate software engineer who has never sewn a quilt.

Maeve and Liam … for oohing and aahing at all of Mommy's creations. The love you have for all your quilts makes my heart melt. I expect Miss Maeve to write her first quilt pattern as soon as she learns to spell "yardage" and "rotary cutter."

Cathy Kirk … for the fabulous quilting and binding on all of the quilts.

Everyone at C&T … for believing in a stay-at-home mom living in the suburbs enough to give me this opportunity.

Susanne Woods … for finding me!

Liz Aneloski … for answering all my millions of questions.

Sandy Peterson … for her amazing attention to detail.

Kristen Yenche and Amy Gonzalez Daniel … for turning my words into a coherent, beautiful book.

Zinnia Heinzmann and Alice Mace Nakanishi … for pulling everything together so smoothly.

Robert Kaufman, Moda, Olfa, and C&T Publishing … for providing fabulous fabric and tools for these projects.

contents

log cabin

FINISHED QUILT SIZE

Crib: 40″ × 50″

Lap: 60″ × 60″

Twin: 68″ × 86″

Queen: 92″ × 88″

Log Cabin 1, 60″ × 60″

Log Cabin blocks are one of the indisputable classics of traditional quilting. If we take this simplicity and go big, we end up with this scrappy skyscraper of log cabins using a variety of strip widths and prints.

fabric selection

When choosing the fabrics, pick 8 unique prints that vary in color and design. You want to have as much contrast as possible among the large concentric loops of color that ring the quilt.

YARDAGE

	Crib	Lap	Twin	Queen
Fabric A	⅞ yard	⅞ yard	1½ yards	1½ yards
Fabric B	⅛ yard	⅝ yard	⅝ yard	⅞ yard
Fabric C	¾ yard	¾ yard	1⅝ yards	1⅝ yards
Fabric D	⅝ yard	⅝ yard	1⅛ yards	1⅛ yards
Fabric E	⅛ yard	¾ yard	¾ yard	1⅝ yards
Fabric F	½ yard	¾ yard	¾ yard	1½ yards
Fabric G	½ yard	½ yard	1¼ yards	1½ yards
Fabric H	⅝ yard	1⅛ yards	1⅛ yards	1½ yards
Binding	½ yard (5 strips)	⅝ yard (7 strips)	¾ yard (9 strips)	⅞ yard (10 strips)
Backing	3 yards	4⅛ yards	5½ yards	8¼ yards
Batting	48″ × 58″	68″ × 68″	76″ × 94″	100″ × 96″

CUTTING

If the Sew First column is checked, then sew together the first cut strips end-to-end and press seams open before making the second cut. A 40″ width of fabric is assumed for calculations. Label your cut pieces with the loop number and size. Be sure to use the Quilt Size column to establish which strips to cut for the size quilt you are making.

Fabric	Loop	Quilt size*	First cut			Second cut	
			Quantity	Size	Sew first	Quantity	Size
A	1	C L T Q	1	4½″ × wof**		1	4½″ × 4½″
	7	C L T Q	2	2½″ × wof		2	2½″ × 20½″
			2	4½″ × wof		2	4½″ × 30½″
	17	T Q	4	3½″ × wof	✓	2	3½″ × 62½″
			4	1½″ × wof	✓	2	1½″ × 74½″
B	2	C L T Q	1	1½″ × wof		2	1½″ × 4½″
						2	1½″ × 6½″
	15	L T Q	3	1½″ × wof	✓	2	1½″ × 56½″
			4	2½″ × wof	✓	2	2½″ × 60½″
	24	Q	5	1½″ × wof	✓	2	1½″ × 88½″
C	3	C L T Q	1	2½″ × wof		2	2½″ × 6½″
						2	2½″ × 10½″
	11	C L T Q	2	3½″ × wof		2	3½″ × 36½″
			3	2½″ × wof	✓	2	2½″ × 50½″
	19	T Q	4	4½″ × wof	✓	2	4½″ × 66½″
			5	1½″ × wof	✓	2	1½″ × 86½″

*C = crib, L = lap, T = twin, Q = queen   **wof = width of fabric

CUTTING CONTINUED

Fabric	Loop	Quilt size*	First cut			Second cut	
			Quantity	Size	Sew first	Quantity	Size
D	4	C L T Q	1	4½″ × wof**		2	4½″ × 10½″
			1	2½″ × wof		2	2½″ × 18½″
	10	C L T Q	4	1½″ × wof	✓	2	1½″ × 34½″
						2	1½″ × 44½″
	18	T Q	4	2½″ × wof	✓	2	2½″ × 64½″
			4	1½″ × wof	✓	2	1½″ × 78½″
E	5	C L T Q	2	1½″ × wof	✓	2	1½″ × 14½″
						2	1½″ × 20½″
	12	L T Q	3	1½″ × wof	✓	2	1½″ × 40½″
			3	4½″ × wof	✓	2	4½″ × 52½″
	20	Q	4	1½″ × wof	✓	2	1½″ × 68½″
			5	4½″ × wof	✓	2	4½″ × 88½″
F	6	C L T Q	1	3½″ × wof		2	3½″ × 16½″
			2	2½″ × wof		2	2½″ × 26½″
	14	L T Q	6	1½″ × wof	✓	2	1½″ × 54½″
						2	1½″ × 58½″
	23	Q	5	4½″ × wof	✓	2	4½″ × 88½″
G	8	C L T Q	2	3½″ × wof		2	3½″ × 28½″
			2	1½″ × wof		2	1½″ × 36½″
	16	T Q	4	4½″ × wof	✓	2	4½″ × 60½″
			4	1½″ × wof	✓	2	1½″ × 68½″
	22	Q	5	1½″ × wof	✓	2	1½″ × 88½″
H	9	C L T Q	2	3½″ × wof		2	3½″ × 30½″
			3	2½″ × wof	✓	2	2½″ × 42½″
	13	L T Q	3	2½″ × wof	✓	2	2½″ × 48½″
			3	3½″ × wof	✓	2	3½″ × 56½″
	21	Q	5	2½″ × wof	✓	2	2½″ × 88½″

*C = crib, L = lap, T = twin, Q = queen   **wof = width of fabric

quilt assembly

Use a precise ¼″ seam allowance while sewing the strips together. Slight variations in the seam width can multiply quickly in this quilt. Press all seams to the outside.

Loops 1 and 2

1. Sew the shorter Loop 2 strips to the top and bottom of the Loop 1 center square. Press. Sew the longer Loop 2 strips to the left and right sides. Press.

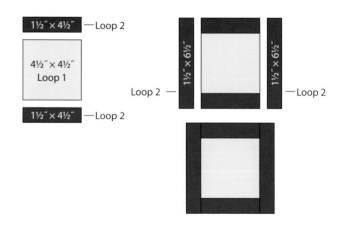

Loop 3

2. Sew the shorter Loop 3 strips to the top and bottom of the unit from Step 1. Press. Sew the longer Loop 3 strips to the left and right sides. Press.

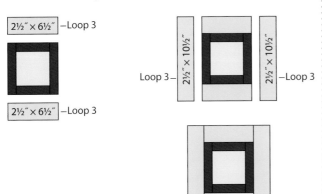

2½″ × 6½″ —Loop 3

2½″ × 6½″ —Loop 3

Loop 3— 2½″ × 10½″

2½″ × 10½″ —Loop 3

3. Continue sewing the loops according to the quilt assembly diagram below, starting with the shorter strips on the top and bottom, pressing, and then sewing the longer strips on the left and right sides and pressing.

Crib: Loops 1–11 *Twin:* Loops 1–19

Lap: Loops 1–15 *Queen:* Loops 1–24

Note: *Loops 21–24 contain strips for the left and right sides only.*

4. Layer, quilt, and bind (see Quiltmaking Basics, pages 58–62).

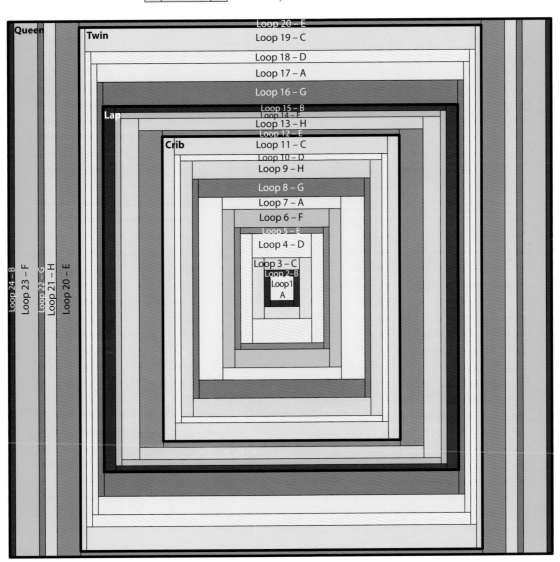

Quilt assembly diagram

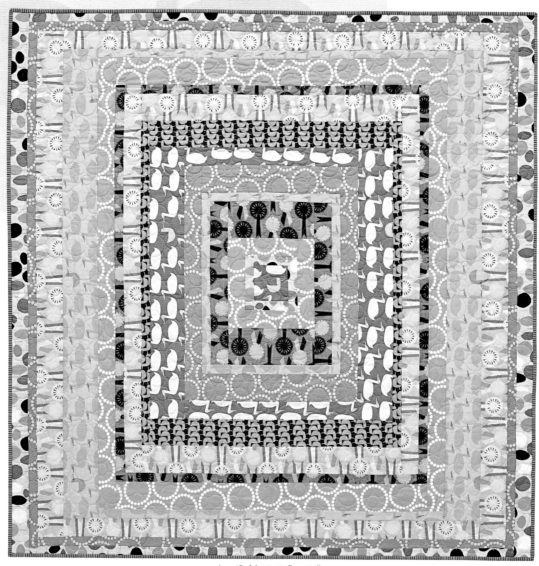

Log Cabin 2, 60″ × 60″

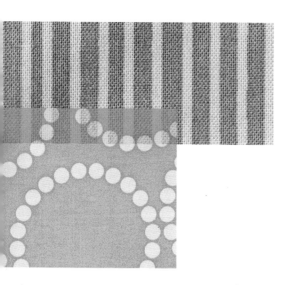

nine patch

FINISHED BLOCK SIZE

7½″ × 7½″

FINISHED QUILT SIZE

Crib: 37½″ × 52½″

Lap: 52½″ × 60″

Twin: 75″ × 90″

Queen: 90″ × 90″

Nine Patch 1, 52½″ × 60″

The traditional Nine-Patch block's strict simplicity can be a pleasant showcase for fabrics. This version injects some whimsy and texture by scattering a second block with stacked circles randomly across the quilt. The print fabric pieces can be cut from yardage or 10″ × 10″ layer cake squares. Requirements for both options are listed in the yardage and cutting charts (page 10).

fabric selection

	Crib	Lap	Twin	Queen
Prints	9 assorted prints ⅜ yard each *or* 35 layer cake squares 10″ × 10″	14 assorted prints ⅜ yard each *or* 56 layer cake squares 10″ × 10″	30 assorted prints ⅜ yard each *or* 120 layer cake squares 10″ × 10″	36 assorted prints ⅜ yard each *or* 144 layer cake squares 10″ × 10″
Solid	1 yard	1⅛ yards	2 yards	2½ yards
Binding	½ yard (6 strips)	⅝ yard (7 strips)	¾ yard (9 strips)	⅞ yard (10 strips)
Backing	2⅞ yards	3¾ yards	7¼ yards	8½ yards
Batting	46″ × 61″	61″ × 68″	83″ × 98″	98″ × 98″

CUTTING

A 40″ width of fabric is assumed for yardage. You can randomly choose which prints to use in each of the two block types, but make sure to have a variety of prints and colors in both types. Be sure to label the sets of your fabric squares with their size.

Quilt size	Prints: Yardage*				Prints: Layer cakes*		Solid			
	First cut (from each print)		Second cut		Trim		First cut		Second cut	
	Quantity	Size	Quantity	Size	Quantity	Size	Quantity	Size	Quantity	Size
Crib	1	10″ × wof**	23	9″ × 9″	23	9″ × 9″	3	8″ × wof	12	8″ × 8″
			12	10″ × 10″	12	No trimming				
Lap	1	10″ × wof	36	9″ × 9″	36	9″ × 9″	4	8″ × wof	20	8″ × 8″
			20	10″ × 10″	20	No trimming				
Twin	1	10″ × wof	80	9″ × 9″	80	9″ × 9″	8	8″ × wof	40	8″ × 8″
			40	10″ × 10″	40	No trimming				
Queen	1	10″ × wof	96	9″ × 9″	96	9″ × 9″	10	8″ × wof	48	8″ × 8″
			48	10″ × 10″	48	No trimming				

*Use **either** yardage **or** layer cakes for print fabric pieces. **wof = width of fabric*

Tip
An Olfa Rotary Circle Cutter makes cutting circles easy (see Resources, page 63).

nine-patch blocks

1. Sort the 9″ × 9″ *print* blocks into sets of about 8 blocks each. When sorting, make sure to evenly distribute the patterns, colors, and design styles. You want each set to be as diverse as possible.

2. Take the first set and spread the squares in a row. Arrange the squares, making sure no matching colors or prints are next to each other. Also, make sure that the first and last squares are different. Stack the squares, aligning the edges for cutting. Repeat for the other sets.

3. Cut through all the layers of each set horizontally and vertically at 3″ intervals to create 9 stacks within each set. Do not disturb the stacks.

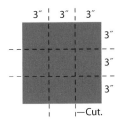

4. Shuffle alternating pieces of the stacks within the block by taking 1 piece from the top of each of the yellow highlighted stacks shown below and moving it to the bottom of its respective stack.

5. Within a set, and using the top pieces from each of the stacks, sew each row together. Press, alternating the direction of the seams in adjacent rows. Then sew the rows together to form a Nine-Patch block. Press.

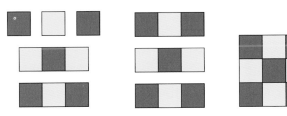

6. Repeat Steps 3–5 with the stacks in the remaining sets to make the following number of Nine-Patch blocks:

Crib: 23   *Lap:* 36   *Twin:* 80   *Queen:* 96

orb blocks

1. From each of the 10″ × 10″ *print* blocks, use a rotary circle cutter to cut 3 circles: 6″, 3½″, and 1½″ in diameter. (Before you cut, add a ¼″ seam allowance all around, if desired, to use the turn-under method of appliqué. Otherwise, plan to raw-edge appliqué the circles in place with no seam allowances.)

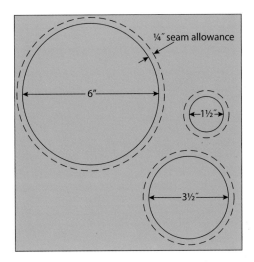

2. For each 8″ *solid* square, pick 3 circles of different prints and sizes and appliqué them onto the square using your preferred method. Make sure the 6″ circle is centered on the solid block and place each smaller circle randomly within.

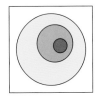

Placement ideas

3. Repeat to make the following number of Orb blocks:

Crib: 12   *Lap:* 20   *Twin:* 40   *Queen:* 48

quilt assembly

1. Arrange the blocks, following the quilt assembly diagram below to assemble the quilt top.

2. Sew the blocks into rows. Press, alternating the directions of seam allowances in adjacent rows.

3. Sew the rows together. Press.

4. Layer, quilt, and bind (see Quiltmaking Basics, pages 58–62).

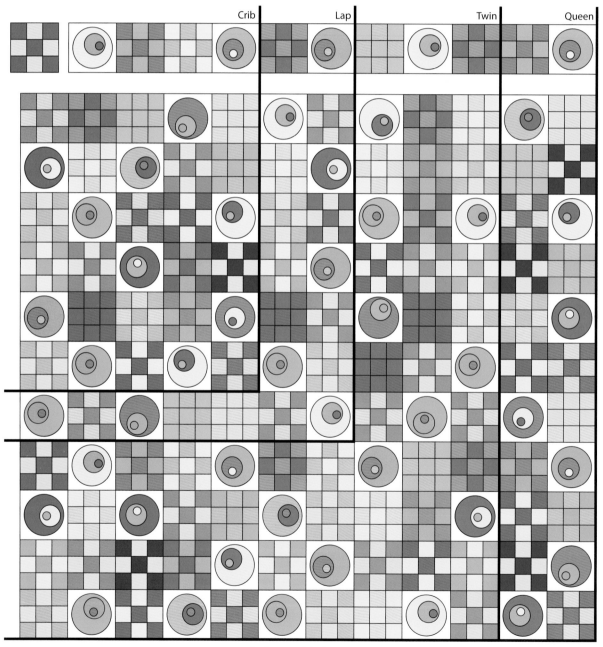

Quilt assembly diagram

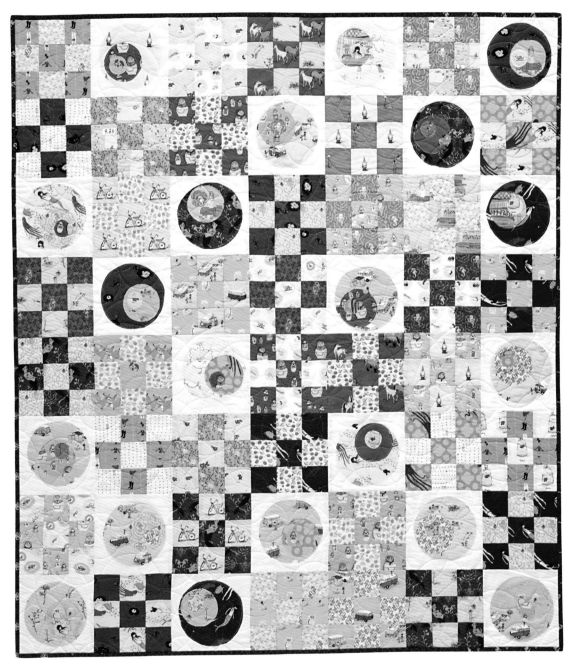

Nine Patch 2, 52½" × 60"

irish chain

FINISHED BLOCK SIZE

7½″ × 7½″

FINISHED QUILT SIZE

Crib: 37½″ × 52½″

Lap: 52½″ × 67½″

Twin: 82½″ × 97½″

Queen: 97½″ × 97½″

Irish Chain 1, 52½″ × 67½″

At first glance, this Irish Chain quilt looks traditional, but then you realize there's something that's just not right. Easy stack-and-cut assembly creates two block styles, which randomly alternate with solid blocks. The print fabric pieces can be cut from yardage or 10″ × 10″ layer cake squares. Requirements for both options are listed in the yardage and cutting charts (page 15).

fabric selection

	Crib	Lap	Twin	Queen
Prints	9 layer cake squares 10″ × 10″ *or* 3 assorted prints ⅜ yard of each	16 layer cake squares 10″ × 10″ *or* 4 assorted prints ⅜ yard of each	36 layer cake squares 10″ × 10″ *or* 9 assorted prints ⅜ yard of each	43 layer cake squares 10″ × 10″ *or* 11 assorted prints ⅜ yard of each
Solid	2¼ yards	3⅛ yards	6⅛ yards	7 yards
Binding	½ yard (6 strips)	⅝ yard (7 strips)	⅞ yard (10 strips)	⅞ yard (11 strips)
Backing	2⅞ yards	3¾ yards	7⅞ yards	9⅛ yards
Batting	46″ × 61″	61″ × 76″	91″ × 106″	106″ × 106″

CUTTING

	Crib	Lap	Twin	Queen
Prints: Layer cakes*	Trim all squares to 9″ × 10″.			
Prints: Yardage*	Cut 1 strip 9″ × wof** from each of the 3 prints; subcut into 9 rectangles 9″ × 10″.	Cut 1 strip 9″ × wof from each of the 4 prints; subcut into 16 rectangles 9″ × 10″.	Cut 1 strip 9″ × wof from each of the 9 prints; subcut into 36 rectangles 9″ × 10″.	Cut 1 strip 9″ × wof from each of the 11 prints; subcut into 43 rectangles 9″ × 10″.
Solid	Cut 3 strips 9″ × wof; subcut into 9 rectangles 9″ × 10″. Cut 4 strips 8″ × wof; subcut into 17 squares 8″ × 8″.	Cut 4 strips 9″ × wof; subcut into 16 rectangles 9″ × 10″. Cut 7 strips 8″ × wof; subcut into 31 squares 8″ × 8″.	Cut 9 strips 9″ × wof; subcut into 36 rectangles 9″ × 10″. Cut 15 strips 8″ × wof; subcut into 71 squares 8″ × 8″.	Cut 11 strips 9″ × wof; subcut into 43 rectangles 9″ × 10″. Cut 17 strips 8″ × wof; subcut into 84 squares 8″ × 8″.

*Use **either** yardage **or** layer cakes for print fabric pieces.   **wof = width of fabric

block assembly

1. Stack the 9″ × 10″ solid and print blocks right sides up into sets of about 8 or 10 pieces each, alternating color and solid pieces. Each set should have an equal number of prints and solids. Line up the edges of the blocks in each set.

Tips

1. It's easiest to work with one set at a time, cutting and sewing the entire set of blocks before moving on to the next.
2. Rotary cut through all the layers at once. It works!

2. Cut the 9″ × 10″ rectangles in a set into 3 strips 3″ × 10″.

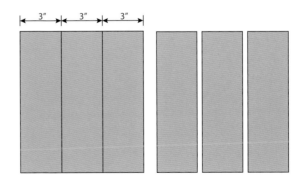

3. Separate the 3 strips slightly, without disturbing the order or the edges.

4. Measure along the long side of each top strip, starting at one end, and mark the lengths with a fabric pen as shown below.

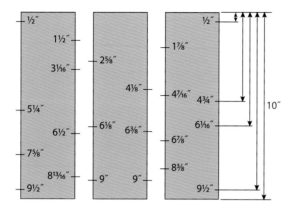

5. Connect the marks, using the fabric pen and a ruler, and cut on the lines. Do not disturb the stacks of pieces.

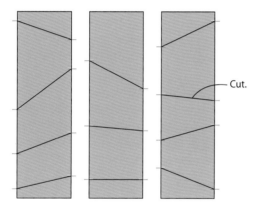

Cut.

6. For each of the yellow-shaded stacks shown below, take 1 piece from the top and move it to the bottom of its respective stack.

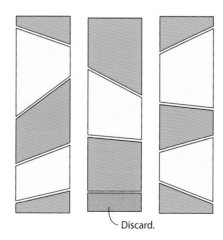

Discard.

Note: *Use a scant ¼″ seam allowance to join the pieces to make the vertical strips of the blocks. This seam allowance is slightly under ¼″ and is necessary to result in an 8″ × 8″ block.*

7. Using the top piece from each stack, sew each strip back together *using a scant ¼″ seam allowance*. Offset the corners of the pieces sewn together to allow for the seam allowance. See note, page 17. Press the seams to one side.

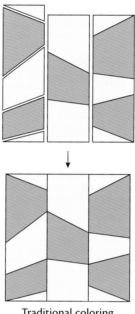

Traditional coloring

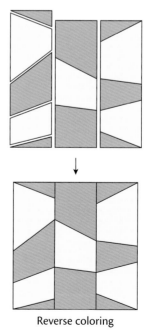

Reverse coloring

Note: *It is easy to offset the corners of the pieces sewn together at an angle. In this case, simply mark the scant ¼″ seam allowance on the wrong sides with a disappearing-ink fabric pen. Line up the seamlines on top of each other with the 2 pieces right sides together, matching the leading seamline endpoints (the end that goes under the presser foot first). The tips of the pieces become naturally offset, and the long sides of the pieces remain straight and aligned when sewn and pressed. Once familiar with the technique, you may be able to skip the marking and simply "eyeball" the correct placement.*

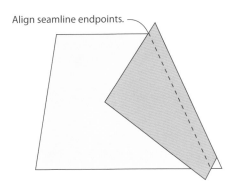

Align seamline endpoints.

8. Sew the 3 vertical strips into the completed quilt block using your regular ¼″ seam allowance. Press, square up the block, and trim to 8″ × 8″. You will have 2 block styles when complete—1 with traditional coloring and 1 with the reverse.

9. Repeat Steps 2–8 with the remaining stacks of pieces in all sets to make the following number of blocks:

Crib: 18   *Lap:* 32   *Twin:* 72   *Queen:* 85

quilt assembly

1. Arrange the pieced and the solid 8″ × 8″ blocks, following the quilt assembly diagram below as a guide. The pieced blocks should have a random color placement and rotation.

2. Sew together the blocks in rows. Press the seams in alternate directions in adjacent rows.

3. Sew the rows together. Press.

4. Layer, quilt, and bind (see Quiltmaking Basics, pages 58–62).

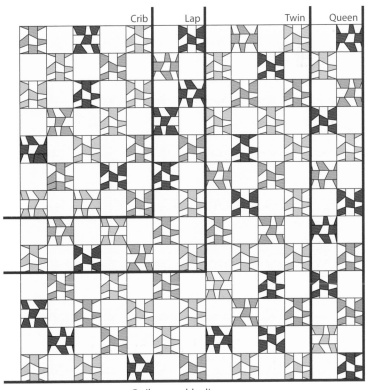

Quilt assembly diagram

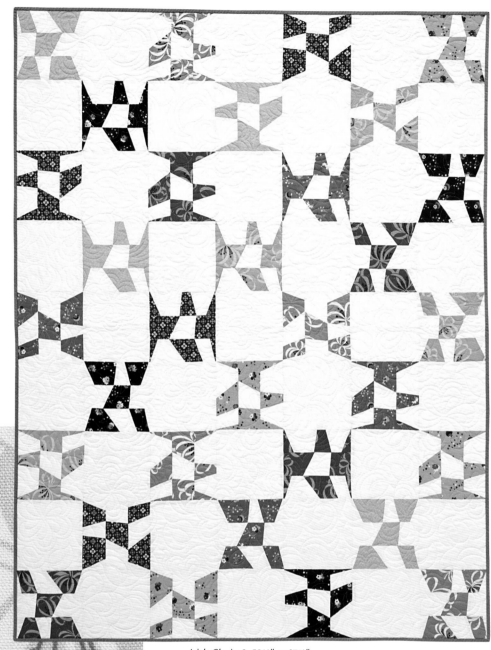

Irish Chain 2, 52½″ × 67½″

storm at sea

FINISHED QUILT SIZE

Crib: 48″ × 48″

Lap: 62″ × 62″

Twin/Queen: 96″ × 96″

Storm at Sea 1, 62″ × 62″

The traditional Storm at Sea blocks are spread over a grid, creating a wavelike optical illusion that almost seems to be moving. This version is a bit of a twister, nesting the blocks inside one another for an entirely different tunnel-like illusion.

For the crib-size quilt, the diamond and corner units in Loops 2–4 form concentric rings around the center square unit (Loop 1). Then, Outer Borders 5B and 6B are added for the lap-size quilt *or* Loop 5TQ is added for the twin/queen-size quilts.

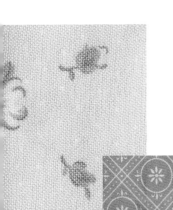

fabric selection

YARDAGE

	Crib	Lap	Twin/Queen
Fabric A (print)	⅜ yard	⅜ yard	⅜ yard
Fabric B (print)	1¼ yards	1¼ yards	1¼ yards
Fabric C (print)	⅝ yard	⅝ yard	3½ yards
Fabric D (print)	1⅞ yards	1⅞ yards	1⅞ yards
Fabric E (print)			5⅝ yards
Fabric F (Border 1)		⅝ yard	
Fabric G (Border 2)		1⅛ yards	
Solid	2⅛ yards	2⅛ yards	6¼ yards
Binding	½ yard (6 strips)	⅝ yard (7 strips)	⅞ yard (11 strips)
Backing	3⅜ yards	4¼ yards	9 yards
Batting	56″ × 56″	70″ × 70″	104″ × 104″

CUTTING

Fabric	Loop number / Placement	Piece name	Number of strips	Size	Cut Quantity	Cut Size
All sizes						
Fabric A (print)	1 / center	AA	1	6½″ × wof*	1	6½″ × 6½″
	3 / corner	EE			4	6½″ × 6½″
Fabric B (print)	2 / diamond	BB	1	3½″ × wof	4	3½″ × 6½″
	4 / corner	GG	2	12½″ × wof	4	12½″ × 12½″
Fabric C (print)	3 / diamond	DD	2	6½″ × wof	4	6½″ × 12½″
Fabric D (print)	2 / corner	CC	1	3½″ × wof	4	3½″ × 3½″
	4 / diamond	FF	4	12½″ × wof	4	12½″ × 24½″
Solid	2 / corner	C1–C4	1	2″ × wof	16	2″ × 2″
	1 / center	A1–A4			4	3½″ × 3½″
	2 / diamond	B1–B4	3	3½″ × wof	8	3½″ × 2⅝″
	3 / corner	E1–E4			16	3½″ × 3½″
	3 / diamond	D1–D4	2	4⅛″ × wof	8	4⅛″ × 6½″
	4 / corner	G1–G4	3	6½″ × wof	16	6½″ × 6½″
	4 / diamond	F1–F4	3	7⅛″ × wof	8	7⅛″ × 12½″

wof = width of fabric

Fabric	Loop number / Placement	Piece name	Number of strips	Size	Cut	
					Quantity	Size
Lap only	*Sew together each set of 6 strips, press seams open, and then subcut.*					
Fabric F (Border 1)	5B		6	2½" × wof	2	2½" × 48½"
					2	2½" × 52½"
Fabric G (Border 2)	6B		6	5½" × wof	2	5½" × 52½"
					2	5½" × 62½"
Twin/Queen only						
Fabric C (print)	5TQ / corner	II	4	24½" × wof	4	24½" × 24½"
Fabric E (print)	5TQ / diamond	HH	4	48½" × wof	4	48½" × 24½"
Solid	5TQ / corner	I1–I4	6	12½" × wof	16	12½" × 12½"
	5TQ / diamond	H1–H4	3	24½" × wof	8	24½" × 13⅛"

*wof = width of fabric

center and corner square units assembly

Refer to the quilt assembly diagrams on pages 23–24 for piece placement. Use the following directions to assemble the center square unit for Loop 1 and the corner square units for Loops 2, 3, 4, and 5TQ.

Align a small solid square in the corner of the larger print square with right sides together. Draw a line from corner to corner on the back of the solid square as shown. Sew on the line and trim, leaving a ¼" seam allowance. Press the seam to the outside. Repeat for the remaining 3 corners.

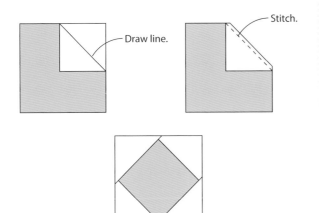

Draw line.

Stitch.

diamond unit assembly

Refer to the quilt assembly diagrams on pages 23–24 for piece placement. Make all markings on the front of the fabric so you don't have to remeasure and mark for the second cut. Use the following directions to assemble the long triangles and center diamond into the diamond units for Loops 2, 3, 4, and 5TQ.

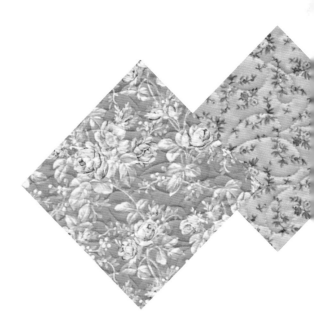

Notes:

1. It is very important to be accurate with your ¼″ seam allowance and to sew in a straight line.

2. Starching the fabric first helps maintain control of the bias edges.

1. To make the long corner triangles for 1 diamond unit, place 2 same-size *solid* rectangles with the wrong sides together. On the short side, mark ⁷⁄₁₆″ from the top left and bottom right corners using a fabric pen. Cut diagonally from mark to mark.

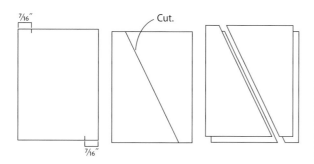

2. On a print rectangle, measure and mark the centers of the long sides. On the short sides, measure and mark ⅛″ above and below the center on both sides. Cut mark-to-mark on 2 opposite corners as shown. Discard these small cut triangles.

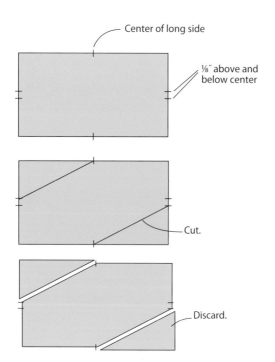

3. Place a solid triangle unit from Step 1 on top of the unit from Step 2, with right sides together, aligning the edge of the blunt end of the triangle with the center mark on the bottom piece. Sew and press the seams to the outside. Repeat for the opposite corner.

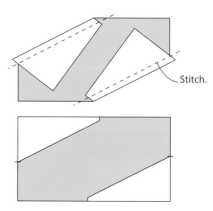

4. Trim mark-to-mark on the remaining 2 corners of the print rectangle in the unit from Step 3, and attach the remaining long solid triangles. Press as you go along.

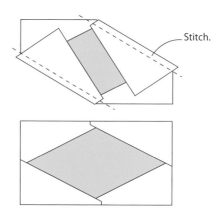

quilt assembly

All Sizes

1. Sew Loop 2 diamond units to both sides of the Loop 1 center square unit. Press the seams open.

2. Make 2 Loop 2 corner-diamond-corner unit rows and sew them to the top and bottom of the unit from Step 1. Press the seams open.

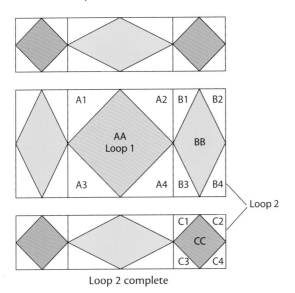

Loop 2 complete

3. Continue as before by adding Loops 3 and 4. The crib-size quilt is now complete. Finish the crib-size quilt by continuing with Step 4. If you would like the quilt to be larger, continue by following either Steps 2–3 in Lap-Size (to the right) or Steps 2–3 in Twin/Queen-Size (page 24).

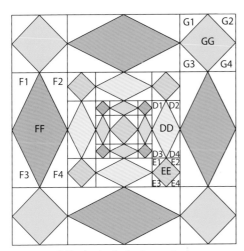

Crib-size includes Loops 1–4.

4. Layer, quilt, and bind (see Quiltmaking Basics, pages 58–62).

Lap-Size

1. Follow Steps 1–3 in All Sizes (to the left).

2. Continue by adding the 2 borders. For Border 1, sew the shorter 5B strips to the left and right sides and press. Then add the longer 5B strips on the top and bottom and press. Repeat for Border 2 using the 6B strips.

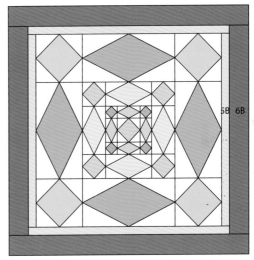

Lap-size includes Loops 1–4 and 2 borders.

3. Layer, quilt, and bind (see Quiltmaking Basics, pages 58–62).

Twin/Queen-Size

1. Follow Steps 1–3 in the section All Sizes (page 23) to make a crib-size quilt.

2. For the twin/queen quilt, do not add the borders (they are used only for the lap-size quilt), but instead add the Loop 5TQ corner and diamond units following the same method for adding loops described for the crib-size quilt (page 23).

3. Layer, quilt, and bind (see Quiltmaking Basics, pages 58–62).

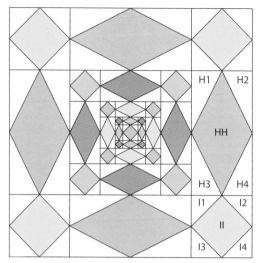

Twin/queen-size includes Loops 1–5.

Storm at Sea 2, 62″ × 62″

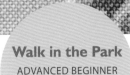

pinwheel

FINISHED QUILT SIZE

Crib: 40″ × 50″

Lap: 50″ × 60″

Twin: 70″ × 90″

Queen: 96″ × 96″

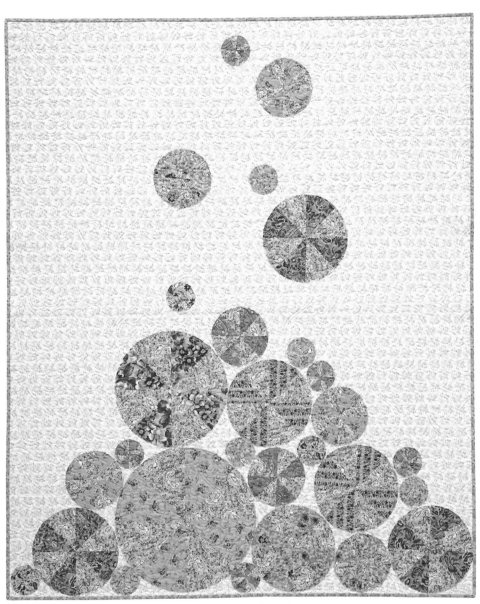

Pinwheel 1, 50″ × 60″

Pinwheels, already a bit of a whimsical pattern, have in this version finally come unstuck entirely and flown away under their own power.

fabric selection

Fabrics from 3 different colorways are used in the pin-wheels. Each colorway has 3–5 different prints using similar colors while still contrasting with each other. (They should contrast with the other colorways but not too much within the colorway.)

The neutral fabric used in the pinwheels can be a solid or a subtle print. It should contrast with all colorways and the background.

The background fabric can be a solid or a subtle tone-on-tone print. It should contrast with all colorways and the neutral in the pinwheels. If you are making the lap-, twin-, or queen-size, avoid large, bold, or other prints that will make the seams obvious when pieced.

Tip
An Olfa Rotary Circle Cutter makes cutting circles easy (see Resources, page 63).

YARDAGE

		Crib	Lap	Twin	Queen
Colorway 1	**Print A**	¼ yard	¼ yard	¼ yard	¼ yard
	Print B	¼ yard	¼ yard	¼ yard	¼ yard
	Print C	⅓ yard	⅓ yard	⅓ yard	⅓ yard
	Print D		½ yard	½ yard	⅝ yard
	Print E				½ yard
Colorway 2	**Print A**	¼ yard	¼ yard	¼ yard	¼ yard
	Print B	¼ yard	¼ yard	⅓ yard	¼ yard
	Print C		⅓ yard	⅓ yard	½ yard
	Print D				½ yard
	Print E	½ yard	½ yard	½ yard	½ yard
Colorway 3	**Print A**	¼ yard	¼ yard	¼ yard	¼ yard
	Print B	¼ yard	¼ yard	¼ yard	⅓ yard
	Print C	⅓ yard	⅓ yard	⅓ yard	½ yard
	Print D			½ yard	½ yard
Neutral		1⅛ yards	1½ yards	1¾ yards	2⅜ yards
Background		1¾ yards*	3¼ yards	5½ yards	8⅞ yards
Backing		3 yards	3½ yards	5¾ yards	9 yards
Binding		½ yard (5 strips)	½ yard (6 strips)	¾ yard (9 strips)	⅞ yard (11 strips)
Batting		48″ × 58″	58″ × 68″	78″ × 98″	104″ × 104″

Minimum 40½″ wof (width of fabric) required.

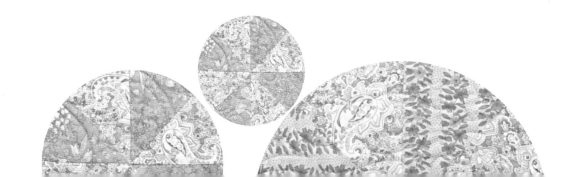

CUTTING

Fabric		Size		Crib		Lap		Twin		Queen	
		First cut (strips)	Second cut (squares)	First cut (# of strips)	Second cut (# of squares)	First cut (# of strips)	Second cut (# of squares)	First cut (# of strips)	Second cut (# of squares)	First cut (# of strips)	Second cut (# of squares)
Colorway 1	Print A	2⅜" × wof*	2⅜" × 2⅜"	1	10	1	10	1	14	2	20
	Print B	3⅞" × wof	3⅞" × 3⅞"	1	4	1	6	1	8	1	8
	Print C	5⅜" × wof	5⅜" × 5⅜"	1	4	1	2	1	6	1	6
	Print D	6⅞" × wof	6⅞" × 6⅞"			1	2	1	4	2	6
	Print E	8⅜" × wof	8⅜" × 8⅜"							1	2
Colorway 2	Print A	2⅜" × wof	2⅜" × 2⅜"	1	4	1	6	1	8	1	8
	Print B	3⅞" × wof	3⅞" × 3⅞"	1	6	1	4	2	12	1	6
	Print C	5⅜" × wof	5⅜" × 5⅜"			1	4	1	4	2	14
	Print D	6⅞" × wof	6⅞" × 6⅞"							1	2
	Print E	8⅜" × wof	8⅜" × 8⅜"	1	2	1	2	1	2	1	2
Colorway 3	Print A	2⅜" × wof	2⅜" × 2⅜"	1	10	1	10	1	12	1	12
	Print B	3⅞" × wof	3⅞" × 3⅞"	1	2	1	4	1	6	2	12
	Print C	5⅜" × wof	5⅜" × 5⅜"	1	2	1	6	1	6	2	8
	Print D	8⅜" × wof	8⅜" × 8⅜"					1	2	1	4
Neutral		2⅜" × wof	2⅜" × 2⅜"	2	24	2	26	3	34	3	40
		3⅞" × wof	3⅞" × 3⅞"	2	12	2	14	3	26	3	26
		5⅜" × wof	5⅜" × 5⅜"	1	6	2	12	3	16	4	28
		6⅞" × wof	6⅞" × 6⅞"			1	2	1	4	2	8
		8⅜" × wof	8⅜" × 8⅜"	1	2	1	2	1	4	2	8
Background**				40½" × 50½"		50½" × 60½"		70½" × 90½"		96½" × 96½"	

*wof = width of fabric   **Background assembly instructions follow.*

background assembly

Crib: Trim the background fabric to 40½" × 50½".

Lap: Cut the fabric in half to form 2 pieces measuring at least 1½ yards each. With right sides together, align the selvages and sew along the selvage edge. Press the seam open and trim to 50½" × 60½".

Twin: Cut the fabric in half to form 2 pieces measuring at least 2⅝ yards each. With right sides together, align the selvages and sew along the selvage edge. Press the seam open and trim to 70½" × 90½".

Queen: Cut the fabric in thirds to form 3 pieces measuring at least 2⅞ yards each. With right sides together, align the selvages of 2 of the pieces and sew along the selvage edge. Repeat for the third piece. Press the seams open and trim to 96½" × 96½".

***Note:** It's not necessary to trim the selvages off first before sewing the background seams since they end up hidden in the seam. Using a ½" seam allowance when assembling the background pieces will allow the seam to lay flatter.*

pinwheel assembly

The assembly method for all the pinwheel appliqués is the same:

1. Take a neutral square and a print square of the same size. Draw a diagonal line with a fabric pen on the wrong side of the neutral square. Place the right sides together and sew with a ¼″ seam allowance on either side of the line. Cut along the diagonal line. Press the seams open. Trim the triangle tails.

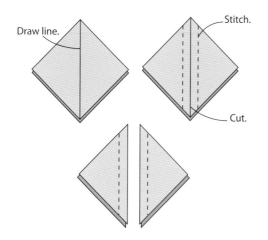

2. Repeat with another pair of neutral and print squares of the same colorway and size to make a total of 4 half-square triangle units.

3. Arrange the 4 newly constructed units, following the illustration below. Sew the top 2 and the bottom 2 units together to form 2 halves. Sew the halves together to form a completed square pinwheel block. Press all the seams open as you sew to reduce bulk.

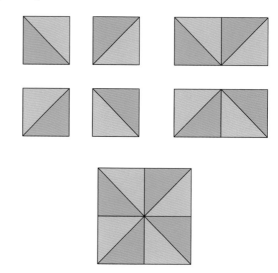

4. Repeat for all the blocks for the size quilt you are making. When completed, you will have the following number of square pinwheel blocks:

Square blocks		Crib	Lap	Twin	Queen
Colorway 1	**Print A:** 3½″	5	5	7	10
	Print B: 6½″	2	3	4	4
	Print C: 9½″	2	1	3	3
	Print D: 12½″		1	2	3
	Print E: 15½″				1
Colorway 2	**Print A:** 3½″	2	3	4	4
	Print B: 6½″	3	2	6	3
	Print C: 9½″		2	2	7
	Print D: 12½″				1
	Print E: 15½″	1	1	1	1
Colorway 3	**Print A:** 3½″	5	5	6	6
	Print B: 6½″	1	2	3	6
	Print C: 9½″	1	3	3	4
	Print D: 15½″			1	2

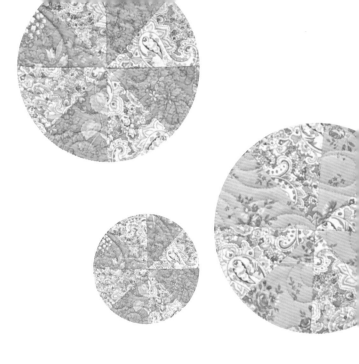

5. Cut the pinwheel square blocks into finished 3″, 6″, 9″, 12″, and 15″ circles (a rotary circle cutter can help with this). Be sure to add your preferred seam allowance all around to these finished sizes before cutting for the turn-under method of appliqué. Cut to these finished sizes if using raw-edge appliqué or other similar method.

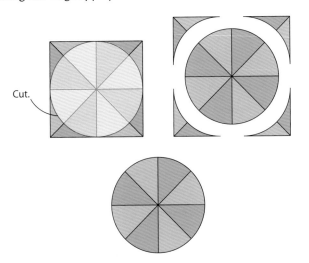

Cut.

quilt assembly

1. Arrange the pinwheel circles on the background fabric according to the illustrations to the right and on page 30. Baste or pin them, making sure the pinwheel circles stay upright (where one seam is vertical). Appliqué the circles onto the background fabric using your favorite method.

> *Note: If making a bed-size quilt to go on a bed with a solid footboard, consider moving the design up so it begins at the foot of the mattress and won't be hidden.*

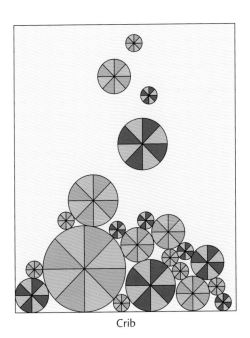

Crib

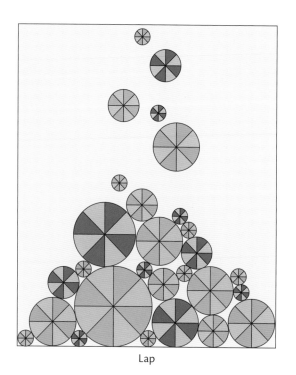

Lap

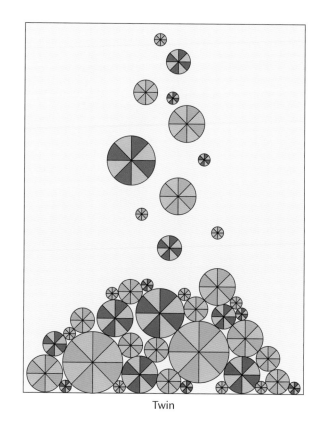

Twin

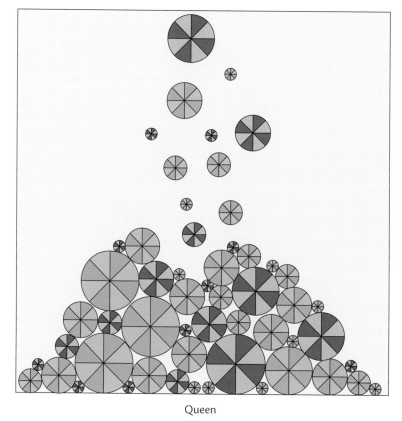

Queen

2. Layer, quilt, and bind (see Quiltmaking Basics, pages 58–62).

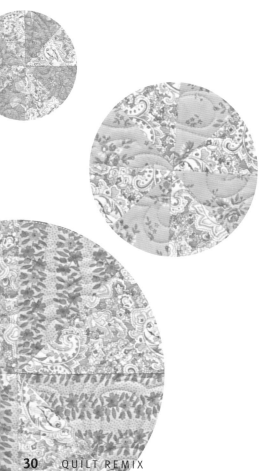

Pinwheel 2, 50″ × 60″

ohio star

FINISHED QUILT SIZE

58½" × 73⅛"

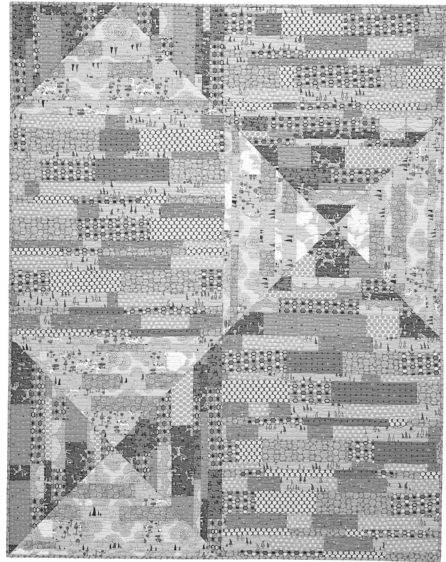

Ohio Star 2, 58½" × 73⅛"

Every quilter knows the feeling: stare at a quilt block for too long, and you start seeing things that aren't there. This zoomed-in Ohio Star block, for instance, features strip piecing and multiple fabrics that we're pretty sure aren't part of most Ohio Stars, no matter how closely you look. They do add a lot of texture though, don't they?

fabric selection

Three fabric colorways make up this supersize macro Ohio Star block quilt. Each colorway is divided into 2 sets, A and B (see cutting charts on pages 34, 35, and 36), with Set A fabrics cut into 1½" and 2½" strips and Set B fabrics cut into 1½" and 3½" strips. About half of the fabrics in each colorway make up a set.

Each colorway has a variety of tones (light, medium, and dark) and print styles (floral, dots, stripes, abstract, and geometric).

Note: It's best for all of the fat quarters within a colorway to be unique, but sometimes that's just not possible. If you do end up with duplicates, put the matching prints in the same set. Have at least 2 unique prints per set when you divide the fat quarters into the sets.

YARDAGE

Colorway 1	13 fat quarters*
Colorway 2	9 fat quarters
Colorway 3	9 fat quarters
Backing	4⅞ yards
Batting	67" × 82"
Binding	⅝ yard (7 strips)

Fat quarters are 18" × 21".

quilt block assembly

Basics

Each colorway has similar instructions for assembly. Read through these instructions first and then follow the specific cutting and sewing instructions for each colorway (pages 34–36).

1. Divide the fat quarters into Sets A and B for each colorway. Press and align the edges of the Set A fat quarters. Trim and square the edges if necessary. Cut strips parallel to the long side of the fat quarter. The quantities and strip widths are given in the charts for the strips for each colorway. Discard any remaining undersized strips.

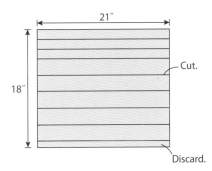

2. Make random vertical cuts in the strips, making sure there are a variety of lengths. Increments of about 2"–10" work well; exact lengths aren't required.

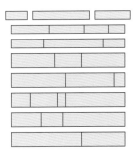

Note: Cut through all the layers at once to keep it simple.

3. Reassemble by sewing the pieces back together randomly to form 1 long patchwork strip for each strip width, keeping the Set A strips separate from the Set B strips. Press seams open or to one side.

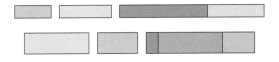

4. Cut the long strips into the quantity and size noted in the cutting chart for each colorway (pages 34–36).

5. Repeat Steps 1–4 for Set B.

6. Assemble the strips into blocks, following the instructions in each colorway (pages 34–36). Press seams open.

Note: Make sure you use an accurate ¼" seam allowance when assembling the strips in the block assemblies, as minor variations in the seam can add up and distort the blocks.

Colorway 1

Following Steps 1–6 in Basics (page 33), cut and reassemble strips for Fabric Sets A and B in Colorway 1 using the specific information in the following cutting chart.

CUTTING

	Set A (6 fat quarters)			Set B (7 fat quarters)		
	Quantity	Size	Name	Quantity	Size	Name
From each fq*, cut (parallel to long side of fq):	3	1½″ × wofq**	—	3	1½″ × wofq	—
	5	2½″ × wofq	—	3	3½″ × wofq	—
After cutting and reassembling, cut long patchwork strips into:	7	1½″ × 29¾″	1A	10	1½″ × 29¾″	1B
	14	2½″ × 29¾″	2A	10	3½″ × 29¾″	3B

*fq = fat quarter   **wofq = width of fat quarter

COLORWAY 1 BLOCK ASSEMBLY

Sew strips together following the illustrations below and on the right to make 2 pieced squares 29¾″ × 29¾″ (trim ¾″, or the amount necessary to make the square, off the top 2A strip) and 1 pieced rectangle 29¾″ × 15⅛″ (trim ⅜″, or the amount necessary to make the rectangle, off the top 1A strip). Press as you sew. Be careful to line up the short ends of the strips as you go along.

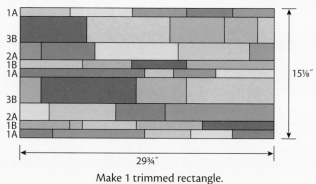

Make 1 trimmed rectangle.

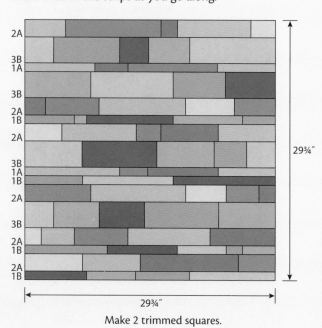

Make 2 trimmed squares.

Colorway 2

Following Steps 1–6 in Basics (page 33), cut and reassemble strips for Fabric Sets A and B in Colorway 2 using the specific information in the following cutting chart.

CUTTING

	Set A (4 fat quarters)			Set B (5 fat quarters)		
	Quantity	Size	Name	Quantity	Size	Name
From each fq*, cut (parallel to long side of fq):	2	1½″ × wofq**	—	3	1½″ × wofq	—
	5	2½″ × wofq	—	3	3½″ × wofq	—
After cutting and reassembling, cut long patchwork strips into:	1	1½″ × 100″	1A	2	1½″ × 100″	1B
	3	2½″ × 100″	2A	2	3½″ × 100″	3B

*fq = fat quarter   **wofq = width of fat quarter*

COLORWAY 2 BLOCK ASSEMBLY

1. Sew strips together following the illustration below to make 1 pieced rectangle 100″ × 15½″.

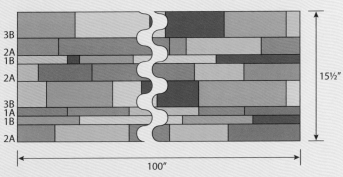

3B
2A
1B
2A
3B
1A
1B
2A

15½″

100″

Make 1 trimmed rectangle.

2. Cut 4 large (30½″ × 15¼″) and 2 small (15½″ × 15½″) triangles, following the illustration below.

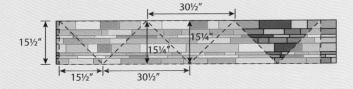

Colorway 3

Following Steps 1–6 in Basics (page 33), cut and reassemble strips for Fabric Sets A and B in Colorway 3 using the specific information in the following cutting chart.

CUTTING

	Set A (4 fat quarters)			Set B (5 fat quarters)		
	Quantity	Size	Name	Quantity	Size	Name
From each fq*, cut (parallel to long side of fq):	4	1½″ × wofq**	—	4	1½″ × wofq	—
	4	2½″ × wofq	—	3	3½″ × wofq	—
After cutting and reassembling, cut long patchwork strips into:	2	1½″ × 100″	1A	3	1½″ × 100″	1B
	2	2½″ × 100″	2A	2	3½″ × 100″	3B

*fq = fat quarter   **wofq = width of fat quarter*

COLORWAY 3 BLOCK ASSEMBLY

1. Sew strips together following the illustration below to make 1 pieced rectangle 15½″ × 100″. Press seams to one side.

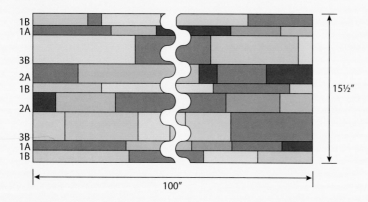

2. Cut 5 large triangles (30½″ × 15¼″), following the illustration below.

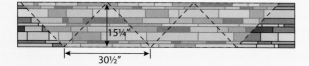

quilt assembly

1. Assemble the quilt top following the illustration below. Sew the triangles from Colorways 2 and 3 together to make 3 blocks, as shown. Press as you sew. Square up and trim the rectangular block made from the triangles to 29¾" × 15⅛".

2. Sew the triangle blocks into 3 rows, alternating with the blocks from Colorway 1. Press.

3. Sew the rows together and press.

4. Layer, quilt, and bind (see Quiltmaking Basics, pages 58–62).

Ohio Star 1, 58½" × 73⅛"

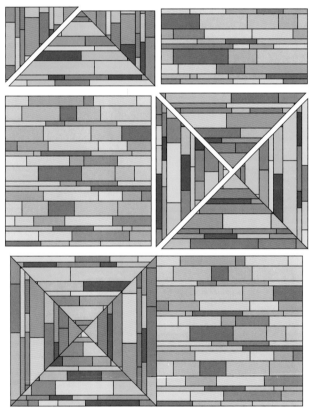

Quilt assembly diagram

trip around the world

FINISHED QUILT SIZE

72″ × 84″

Trip Around the World 1, 72″ × 84″

The traditional Trip Around the World is striking but a touch too straightforward. Add in a few more worlds, though, and things start to get interesting.

fabric selection

Pick 3 contrasting colorways. Within each colorway, select 4 prints that vary slightly for texture. Solids or very small prints work best for this quilt.

YARDAGE

	Colorway 1	Colorway 2	Colorway 3
Print / Color A	1⅛ yards	¾ yard	¾ yard
Print / Color B	¾ yard	¾ yard	⅝ yard
Print / Color C	⅞ yard	¾ yard	⅝ yard
Print / Color D	¾ yard	1 yard	⅝ yard
Binding	¾ yard (9 strips)		
Backing	5⅜ yards		
Batting	80″ × 92″		

CUTTING

Cut each fabric into the specified number of 2½″-wide strips. Subcut the 2½″ strips into second-cut pieces, cutting the longest pieces first, then the next longest, and so on until all the pieces have been cut.

Print/Color	Colorway 1				Colorway 2				Colorway 3			
	1A	1B	1C	1D	2A	2B	2C	2D	3A	3B	3C	3D
First cut												
Number of 2½″ × wof* strips	13	8	10	8	9	8	9	11	9	7	5	7
Second cut												
36½″			1				1					
32½″	1		1					1				
30½″			1						1			
28½″	1			1	1					1		
26½″								2		1		1
24½″		3				2	1				1	1
22½″					1	1			1			
20½″	3				1		2		2	1	1	1
18½″	2	1	1			1		2	2	1	1	2
16½″	1		3		2			2	1	1		1
14½″	2	1	1	2	1	2	1	3	1		1	1
12½″			2	3	2	2		2		2	2	
10½″		2										
8½″	4	2					6			2	2	
4½″	2	2		2	2	4						4
2½″	81	42	66	53	48	38	44	54	33	26	23	30

wof = width of fabric

quilt assembly

1. Working with the pieces of the first section shown in the quilt assembly diagram (below), sew each row together. When all 7 rows of the first section are complete, sew the rows together. Press the seams open as you go along. Be careful to line up the ends of the rows so the section stays rectangular.

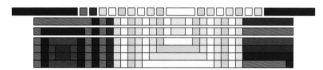

Note: It's important to have an accurate ¼″ seam when sewing the rows so the quilt doesn't end up skewed. Make sure you don't pull the fabric when pressing.

2. Repeat for the remaining 5 sections.

3. Sew the completed sections together. Press.

4. Layer, quilt, and bind (see Quiltmaking Basics, pages 58–62).

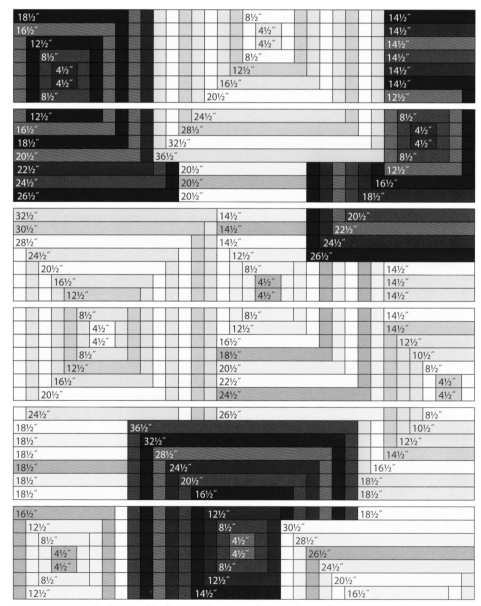

Quilt assembly diagram. Cut sizes of pieces shown for placement.
Where no piece size is designated, use a piece 2½″ long.

Trip Around the World 2, 72" × 84"

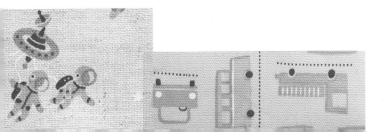

dresden plate

Walking Uphill …
Both Ways …
In the Snow
INTERMEDIATE PROJECT

FINISHED BLOCK SIZE

15″ × 15″

FINISHED QUILT SIZE

Crib: 45″ × 60″

Lap: 60″ × 60″

Twin: 75″ × 90″

Queen: 90″ × 90″

Dresden Plate 1, 60″ × 60″

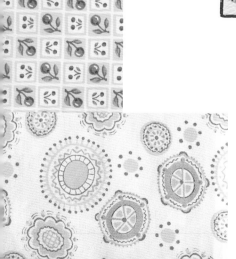

This hard-edged Dresden Plate uses contrast and angles to bring an entirely new look without changing the structure of the classic pattern.

fabric selection

There should be a stark contrast between the solids and prints and between the prints themselves. The chart lists the minimum number of prints needed, but additional prints may be used for more variety. Precut 10″ × 10″ layer cake squares may be used instead and will give an even wider variety.

YARDAGE

	Crib	Lap	Twin	Queen
Prints	6 assorted prints ⅓ yard of each *or* 24 layer cake squares 10″ × 10″	8 assorted prints ⅓ yard of each *or* 32 layer cake squares 10″ × 10″	15 assorted prints ⅓ yard of each *or* 60 layer cake squares 10″ × 10″	18 assorted prints ⅓ yard of each *or* 72 layer cake squares 10″ × 10″
Solid	2 yards	2½ yards	4½ yards	5⅜ yards
Backing	3¼ yards	4⅛ yards	7¼ yards	8½ yards
Batting	53″ × 68″	68″ × 68″	83″ × 98″	98″ × 98″
Binding	½ yard (6 strips)	⅝ yard (7 strips)	⅞ yard (10 strips)	⅞ yard (10 strips)

CUTTING

No additional cutting is needed for the layer cake squares.

Quilt size	Prints				Solid			
	First cut (*from each print*)		Second cut		First cut		Second cut	
	Quantity	Size	Quantity	Size	Quantity	Size	Quantity	Size
Crib	1	10″ × wof*	24	10″ × 10″	6	10″ × wof	24	10″ × 10″
Lap	1		32		8		32	
Twin	1		60		15		60	
Queen	1		72		18		72	

wof = width of fabric

block assembly

1. Sort the 10″ print squares into roughly equal stacks of at least 5 squares each. When sorting, make sure to evenly distribute the patterns, colors, and design styles. You want each stack to be as diverse as possible.

2. Take the first stack and spread the squares into a row. Arrange the squares, making sure no 2 matching colors or prints are next to each other and that the first and last squares are different. Stack the squares, aligning the edges for cutting. Repeat for the other stacks.

3. Add to the top of each stack the *same number* of solid 10″ squares as there are prints in that stack.

Note: It's easiest to work with 1 stack at a time, cutting and sewing the entire set of blocks before moving on to the next stack. In the illustrations for this project, pieces shaded white represent the solid-colored pieces.

4. Using a rotary cutter, make 4 random cuts per stack, following one of the illustrations on page 44 as a guide, to make 5 sets of strips per stack.

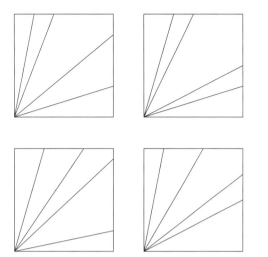

5. Separate the 5 sets of strips slightly. Make a random diagonal cut in each set of strips to divide them into inner and outer segments; follow the illustrations below as guides. Don't disturb the sets of strips.

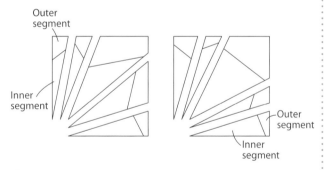

6. While maintaining their layout and order, remove all of the *solid inner segment* pieces from the top of the sets of strips and the *print outer segment* pieces from the bottoms of the sets of strips. Move these pieces to the side and place them in their same relative positions to make Block A.

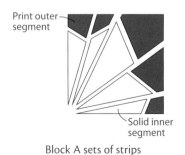

Block A sets of strips

7. The remaining *solid outer segment* pieces from the tops of the sets of strips and the *print inner segment* pieces from the bottoms of the sets of strips form Block B.

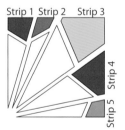

Block B sets of strips

8. Shuffle the *print outer segment* pieces in each set of strips in Block A to create a random fabric arrangement as follows:

a. Leave Strip 1 as it is.

b. Take 1 piece from the top of Strip 2 and move it to the bottom of that set.

c. Take 2 pieces from the top of Strip 3 and move them to the bottom of that set.

d. Take 3 pieces from the top of Strip 4 and move them to the bottom of that set.

e. Take 4 pieces from the top of Strip 5 and move them to the bottom of that set.

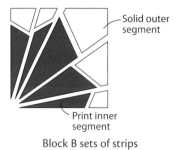

Shuffled sets of strips Block A

9. Repeat for the *print inner segment* pieces of Block B.

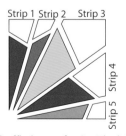

Shuffled sets of strips Block B

10. Starting with the top pieces of Strip 1 in Block A, place the outer segment piece on top, offset the leading corner to allow for the ¼″ seam allowance, and sew it to the adjacent inner segment piece, keeping the right sides together. Press the seam allowance toward the darker fabric and trim the edges.

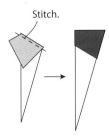

Stitch.

Note: **To offset the leading corner when joining the inner and outer segments, mark the seamlines of both pieces on the wrong side of the fabric. With the outer segment piece on top and with right sides together, line up the seamlines on top of each other, matching their leading endpoints. (This is the end of the seam where stitching starts.) Sew on the seamlines, and the top piece will be naturally offset. The trailing edges (at the end of the seam) will not be aligned, because the original strip is now smaller. Once you are comfortable with the procedure, you may be able to eyeball the offset amount and skip marking the seamlines. See the note in Block Assembly, Irish Chain (page 17), for more information.**

11. Repeat Step 10 for the other top pieces of the 4 strips in Block A.

12. Sew the top 5 strips together, starting with Strips 1 and 2 and then 3 and 4. Then sew Strip 5 to Strips 3/4 and finish by sewing Strips 1/2 to Strips 3/4/5. Again, offset the strips to accommodate the seam allowance so the strips stay aligned along the outer edges of the block. Press the seam allowances open to help reduce the bulk in the center of the block. Be careful not to stretch the bias-cut edges.

13. Trim the block to 8″ square.

Trim.

14. Repeat Steps 4–13 with the remaining stacks to make the following number of blocks:

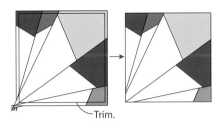

Block A   *Crib:* 24   *Lap:* 32   *Twin:* 60   *Queen:* 72

Block B   *Crib:* 24   *Lap:* 32   *Twin:* 60   *Queen:* 72

quilt assembly

1. Sew a Block A to a Block B. Press the seam allowances open. Repeat. Sew the 2 units together to form a final block as shown below. Press. Make the following number of final blocks:

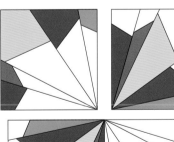

Crib: 12   *Lap:* 16   *Twin:* 30   *Queen:* 36

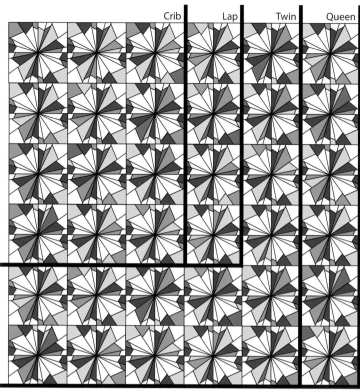

Crib | Lap | Twin | Queen

Quilt assembly diagram

2. Sew the blocks into rows following the quilt assembly diagram (to the left). Press the seam allowances in different directions in adjacent rows. Try not to place blocks with the same original cuts adjacent to each other in this step.

3. Layer, quilt, and bind (see Quiltmaking Basics, pages 58–62).

Dresden Plate 2, 60" × 60"

lone star

FINISHED QUILT SIZE

Crib: 38″ × 55½″

Lap: 53½″ × 55½″

Twin: 68½″ × 92½″

Queen: 91½″ × 92½″

Lone Star 1, 53½″ × 55½″

This version of the Lone Star has been deconstructed down to its basic elements and built back up into a lattice pattern, in the process avoiding the original's difficult seams.

fabric selection

The quilt is made from 3 colorways, using several prints from each colorway. Fabrics with little contrast in the print work best.

YARDAGE

	Crib			Lap			Twin			Queen		
	CW*1	CW2	CW3	CW1	CW2	CW3	CW1	CW2	CW3	CW1	CW2	CW3
Half- and quarter-diamonds (A, B, Br)	⅜ yard each of 2 prints	⅜ yard each of 4 prints	⅜ yard each of 3 prints	⅜ yard each of 3 prints	⅜ yard each of 5 prints	⅜ yard each of 3 prints	⅜ yard each of 5 prints	⅝ yard each of 4 prints	⅝ yard each of 4 prints	⅝ yard each of 4 prints	⅞ yard each of 4 prints	⅞ yard each of 3 prints
Sashing (C, Cr)	⅞ yard			1⅛ yards			2⅛ yards			2⅞ yards		
Cornerstones (D)	¼ yard			¼ yard			½ yard			½ yard		
Backing	2⅞ yards			3¾ yards			5⅞ yards			8⅝ yards		
Batting	46" × 64"			62" × 64"			77" × 101"			100" × 101"		
Binding	½ yard (6 strips)			⅝ yard (7 strips)			¾ yard (9 strips)			⅞ yard (11 strips)		

*CW = colorway

CUTTING

Keep the fabric folded on the manufacturer's fold so Piece B and its reverse (Br) and Piece C and its reverse (Cr) can be cut at the same time.

Note: *The fast2cut Half- & Quarter-Diamond Rulers (see Resources, page 63) make cutting the half- and quarter-diamonds easy.*

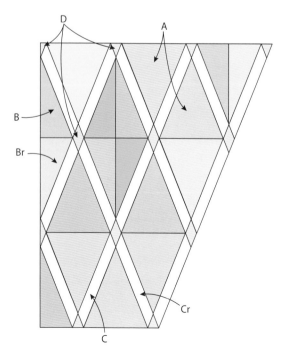

CUTTING

	Crib			Lap			Twin			Queen		
Half- and quarter-diamonds (A, B, Br)												
First cut (8¾" × wof* strips)	CW**1/2/3: 1 strip from each print						**CW1:** 1 strip from each print; **CW2/3:** 2 strips from each print			**CW1:** 2 strips from each print; **CW2/3:** 3 strips from each print		
Second cut*	*Type/number of pieces to cut*												
	A	B	Br	A	B	Br	A	B	Br	A	B	Br
Colorway 1	2	2	2	13	5	5	33	11	11	45	21	21
Colorway 2	20	12	12	32	8	8	53	19	19	71	23	23
Colorway 3	19	5	5	19	7	7	40	24	24	56	24	24
Sashing (C, Cr)												
First cut	15 strips 1⁹⁄₁₆" × wof			21 strips 1⁹⁄₁₆" × wof			45 strips 1⁹⁄₁₆" × wof			60 strips 1⁹⁄₁₆" × wof		
Second cut	C		Cr	C		Cr	C		Cr	C		Cr
	30			42			90			120		
Cornerstones (D)												
First cut	3 strips 1⁹⁄₁₆" × wof			4 strips 1⁹⁄₁₆" × wof			7 strips 1⁹⁄₁₆" × wof			9 strips 1⁹⁄₁₆" × wof		
Second cut	38			52			104			138		

*wof = width of fabric   **CW = colorway   ***A summary of the method used to make the second cuts follows this chart.*

Half- and Quarter-Diamonds (A, B, and Br)

Using the fast2cut Half- & Quarter-Diamond Ruler Set, or the measurements shown in the illustration (below), cut Pieces A, B, and Br from the 8¾" strips. Start at the selvage edge and cut the B and Br quarter-diamonds. Then cut the A half-diamonds. Make sure to cut A, B, and Br pieces from each print. Remember to allow for the ¼" top edge of Pieces B and Br as you cut them.

Note: Half-diamonds on the edges of the quilt may change from an A piece to quarter-diamond B or Br pieces, or vice versa, depending on the size quilt you are making. See the quilt assembly diagram (page 51) for clarification.

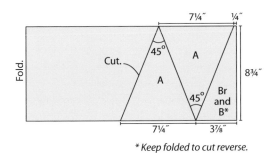

* Keep folded to cut reverse.

C and Cr Sashing

Cut the 1⁹⁄₁₆" strips at 45° in 9¼" increments.

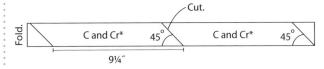

* Keep folded to cut reverse.

D Cornerstones

Cut the 1⁹⁄₁₆" strips at 45° in 2³⁄₁₆" increments.

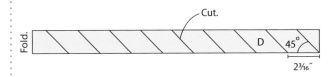

diamond and half-diamond assembly

Following the chart and illustrations below, assemble A, B, and Br pieces into diamonds and half-diamonds. Use different prints within the same colorway to make the diamonds and half-diamonds. Press all seams to one side. Any leftover pieces will be used as single pieces in the quilt-top assembly.

	A/A			B–Br / Br–B			B / Br			B–Br		
	CW*1	CW2	CW3	CW1	CW2	CW3	CW1	CW2	CW3	CW1	CW2	CW3
Crib	1	8	8		4	2		4				1
Lap	5	14	8		4	2	4				1	1
Twin	15	24	19	4	6	9		4	4	1	3	2
Queen	19	33	25	8	9	9	4	2	4	1	3	2

*CW = colorway

A/A

Select 2 A half-diamonds, place them with their right sides together, and sew along the short side.

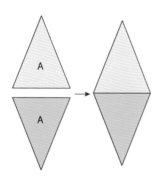

B/Br

Place a B and a Br quarter-diamond with right sides together and sew along the short side.

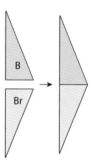

B–Br / Br–B

Place a B and a Br quarter-diamond right sides together and sew along the long leg of the right angle. Repeat. Sew the 2 units together with right sides together to form the completed diamond.

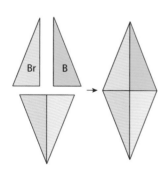

B–Br

Place a B and a Br quarter-diamond with right sides together and sew along the long leg of the right angle.

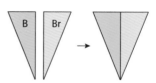

quilt assembly

1. Following the quilt assembly diagram and the detail shown below, sew diagonal rows, alternating the half-, quarter-, and full-diamond units with Sashing Strips Cr as shown. Press the seam allowances to one side. Sew adjacent diagonal rows by alternating Sashing Strips C with Cornerstones D, as shown. Press seam allowances to the other side.

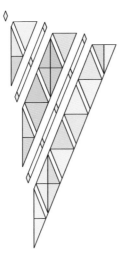

2. Sew the rows together to form the completed quilt top. Ease in any slight fullness in the triangles or the cornerstones. Press.

3. Trim the cornerstone overage.

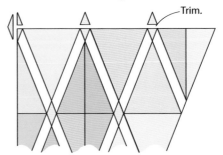

4. Layer, quilt, and bind (see Quiltmaking Basics, pages 58–62).

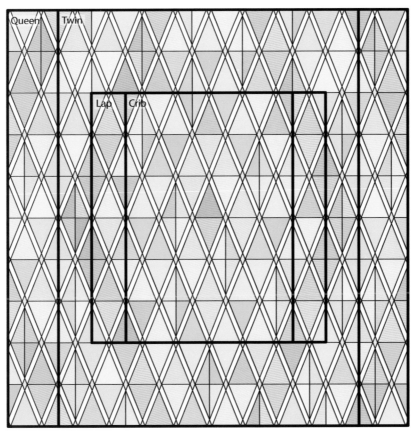

Quilt assembly diagram

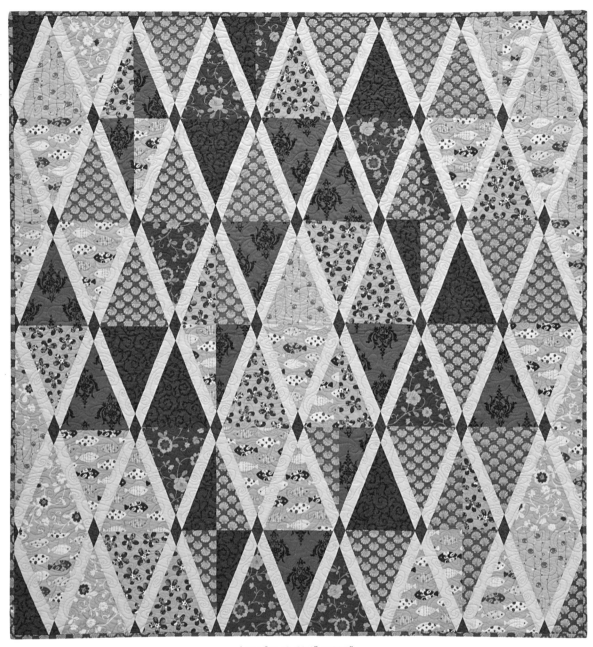

Lone Star 2, 53½″ × 55½″

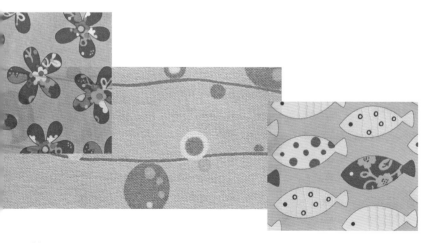

flying geese

FINISHED QUILT SIZE

81″ × 81″

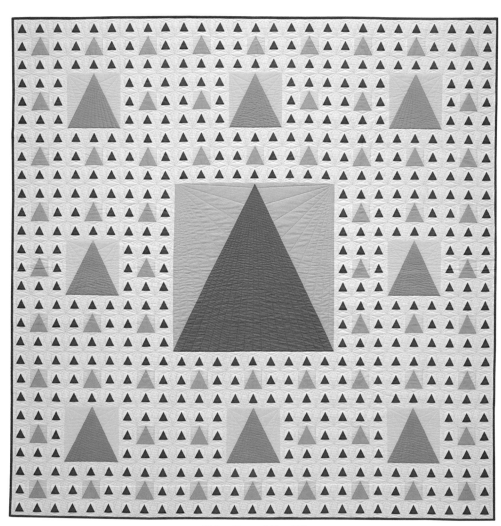

Flying Geese, 81″ × 81″

Flying Geese quilts are traditionally very geometric, with orderly designs. This quilt takes the order to another level entirely by arranging square versions of a Flying Geese block in mathematical precision.

Note: *If you are curious, this pattern follows the Sierpinski carpet fractal. Those aren't typos in the cutting chart! This quilt is made of 3,803 pieces, almost all of which are easily foundation pieced.*

fabric selection

YARDAGE

Background		7¼ yards
Solid 1	Dark	2⅛ yards
	Light	2⅞ yards
Solid 2	Dark	1 yard
	Light	1⅛ yards
Solid 3	Dark	1 yard
	Light	1 yard
Solid 4	Dark	1 yard
	Light	1 yard
Backing		7⅝ yards
Batting		89″ × 89″
Binding		¾ yard

Notes:

1. Quilter's Freezer Paper Sheets or Carol Doak's Foundation Paper (see Resources, page 63) make paper piecing easy.

2. These foundation pieces are cut with a ⅜″ seam allowance all around, for ease of paper piecing.

3. Use your favorite method to foundation piece these blocks.

block assembly

Block A

Photocopy or trace the foundation pattern on page 55 and make 512 of Block A, using Solid 1 (dark and light) and background fabrics placed as shown in the following illustration. Trim blocks, leaving a ¼″ seam allowance all around (3½″ × 3½″). Remove the foundation paper.

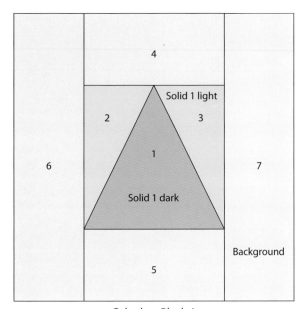

Color key, Block A

CUTTING

Fabric		First cut		Second cut			Placement	
		Quantity	Size	Quantity	Pieces per strip	Size	Block	Piece(s)
Background		164	1½″ × wof*	1,024	17	2¼″ × 1½″	A	4, 5
				1,024	10	3¾″ × 1½″	A	6, 7
Solid 1	Dark	31	2¼″ × wof	512	17	2¼″ × 2¼″	A	1
	Light	64	1½″ × wof	1,024	16	2½″ × 1½″	A	2, 3
Solid 2	Dark	7	3¾″ × wof	64	10	3¾″ × 3¾″	B	1
	Light	15	2¼″ × wof	128	9	4⅛″ × 2¼″	B	2, 3
Solid 3	Dark	2	9½″ × wof	8	4	9½″ × 9½″	C	Inner
	Light	2	9½″ × wof	16	8	5″ × 9½″	C	Outer
Solid 4	Dark	1	27½″ × wof	1	1	27½″ × 27½″	D	Inner
	Light	1	27½″ × wof	2	2	14″ × 27½″	D	Outer

*wof = width of fabric

Block B

1. Photocopy or trace the foundation pattern (below) and make 64 Block B center triangles, using Solid 2 (dark and light) fabrics placed as shown in the following illustration. Trim blocks, leaving a ¼″ seam allowance all around (3½″ × 3½″). Remove foundation paper.

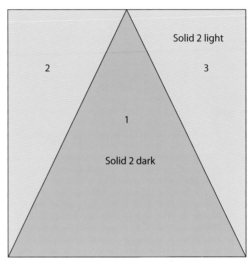

Color key, Block B center triangle

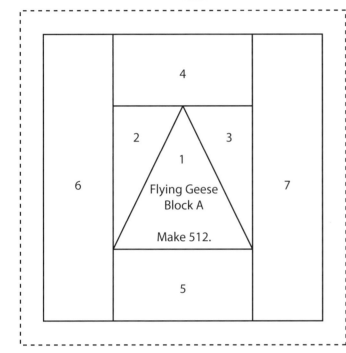

Block A pattern

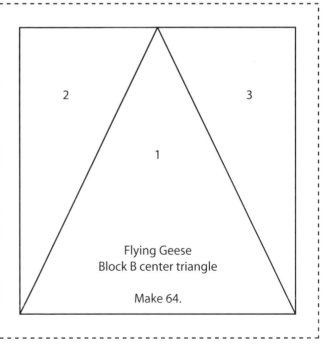

Block B center triangle pattern

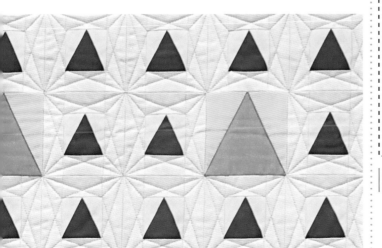

2. Arrange 8 Block A units and 1 Block B center triangle unit following the illustration below. Sew the blocks into 3 rows and then sew the 3 rows together to form a completed Block B. Press all seams open as you sew.

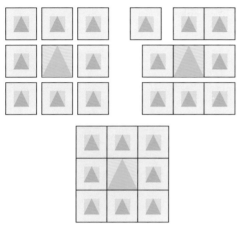

Make Block B.

3. Repeat to make 64 of Block B.

Block C

1. Make 8 Block C center triangles using Solid 3 (dark and light). For the left side triangle, mark 8 Solid 3 light 5″ × 9½″ rectangles ⅜″ in on both sides, as shown in the following illustration. Draw a line joining the pair of marks. Cut on the line and discard the piece, as shown.

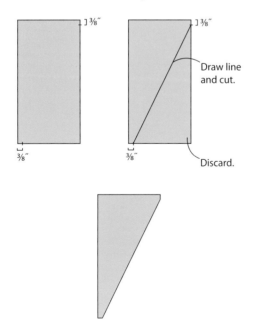

2. For the right side triangle, cut the remaining 8 Solid 3 light 5″ × 9½″ rectangles as shown below.

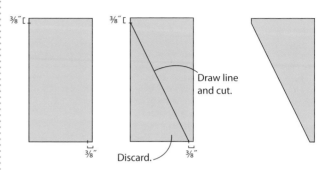

3. Make 2 marks along the top of each of the 9½″ Solid 3 dark squares ¼″ to each side of center. Line up the left triangle on top of the square, right sides together, offsetting the triangle to allow for a ¼″ seam allowance. The left triangle seam allowance lines up with the right-hand ¼″ mark and vice versa. Pin and sew. Trim the excess and press the seam toward the outside. Repeat on the right side.

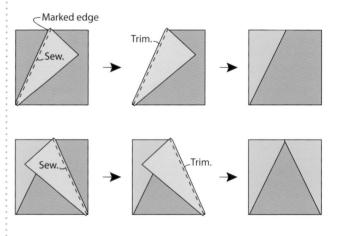

Note: **To offset the triangles when sewing to the square, mark the seamlines on the wrong side of the pieces. With right sides together, align the bottom corner seamlines of both pieces. At the top of the block, align the ⅜″ mark on the triangle with the near side ¼″ mark of the square. Sew along the long edge of the triangle, using a ¼″ seam allowance. Once you are comfortable with the procedure, you may be able to eyeball the offset amount. For more information, see the note in Block Assembly, Irish Chain (page 17).**

4. Arrange 8 of Block B and 1 Block C center triangle following the illustration below. Sew the blocks into 3 rows and sew the 3 rows together to form a completed Block C. Press all seams open as you sew.

5. Repeat Step 4 to make 8 of Block C.

Block D and Quilt Assembly

1. Make 1 Block D center triangle using 2 Solid 4 light pieces and 1 dark piece following the method explained in Block C (Steps 1–3, page 56).

2. Arrange 8 Block C and 1 Block D center triangle, following the quilt assembly diagram (below). Sew the blocks into 3 rows and then sew the 3 rows together to form the completed quilt top. Press all seams open as you sew.

3. Layer, quilt, and bind (see Quiltmaking Basics, pages 58–62).

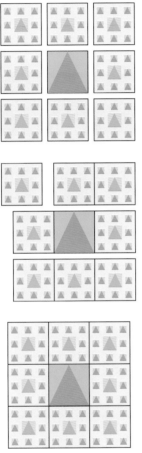

Make Block C.

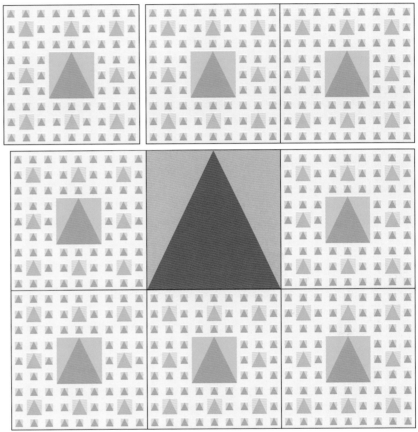

Quilt assembly diagram

quiltmaking basics
HOW TO FINISH YOUR QUILT

general guidelines

Seam Allowances

A ¼″ seam allowance is used for most projects, unless noted otherwise. It's a good idea to do a test seam before you begin sewing to check that your ¼″ is accurate. Accuracy is the key to successful piecing.

There is no need to backstitch. Seamlines will be crossed by another seam, which will anchor them.

Pressing

In general, press seams toward the darker fabric, unless noted otherwise. Press lightly in an up-and-down motion. Avoid using a very hot iron or over-ironing, which can distort shapes and blocks. Be especially careful when pressing bias edges, as they stretch easily.

Backing

Plan on making the backing a minimum of 8″ longer and wider than the quilt top. Piece, if necessary.

To economize, piece the back from any leftover quilting fabrics or blocks in your collection.

Batting

The type of batting to use is a personal decision; consult your local quilt shop. Cut batting approximately 8″ longer and wider than your quilt top. Note that your batting choice will affect how much quilting is necessary for the quilt. Check the manufacturer's instructions to see how far apart the quilting lines can be.

Layering

Spread the backing wrong side up and tape the edges down with masking tape. (If you are working on carpet, you can use T-pins to secure the backing to the carpet.) Center the batting on top, smoothing out any folds. Place the quilt top right side up on top of the batting and backing, making sure it is centered.

Basting

Basting keeps the quilt "sandwich" layers from shifting while you are quilting.

If you plan to machine quilt, pin baste the quilt layers together with safety pins placed a minimum of 3"–4" apart. Begin basting in the center and move toward the edges, first in vertical, then horizontal rows. Try not to pin directly on the intended quilting lines.

If you plan to hand quilt, baste the layers together with thread, using a long needle and light-colored thread. Knot one end of the thread. Using stitches approximately the length of the needle, begin in the center and move out toward the edges in vertical and horizontal rows approximately 4" apart. Add 2 diagonal rows of basting.

Quilting

Quilting, whether by hand or machine, enhances the pieced or appliquéd design of the quilt. You may choose to quilt in-the-ditch, echo the pieced or appliqué motifs, use patterns from quilting design books and stencils, or do your own free-motion quilting. Remember to check your batting manufacturer's recommendations for how close the quilting lines must be.

Binding

Trim excess batting and backing from the quilt even with the edges of the quilt top.

DOUBLE-FOLD STRAIGHT GRAIN BINDING

If you want a generous ¼" finished binding, cut the binding strips 2½" wide and piece them together with diagonal seams to make a continuous binding strip. Trim the seam allowance to ¼". Press the seams open.

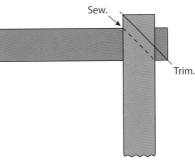

Sew from corner to corner.

Completed diagonal seam

Press the entire strip in half lengthwise with wrong sides together. With raw edges even, pin the binding to the front edge of the quilt a few inches away from the corner and leave the first few inches of the binding unattached. Start sewing, using a ¼" seam allowance.

Stop ¼" away from the first corner (see Step 1) and backstitch 1 stitch. Lift the presser foot and needle. Rotate the quilt one-quarter turn. Fold the binding at a right angle so it extends straight above the quilt and the fold forms a 45° angle in the corner (see Step 2). Then bring the binding strip down even with the edge of the quilt (see Step 3). Begin sewing at the folded edge. Repeat in the same manner at all corners.

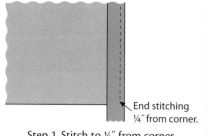

Step 1. Stitch to ¼″ from corner.

End stitching ¼″ from corner.

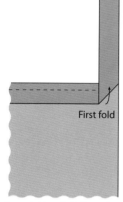

First fold

Step 2. First fold for miter

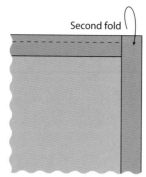

Second fold

Step 3. Second fold alignment

Continue stitching until you are back near the beginning of the binding strip. See Finishing the Binding Ends (page 61) for tips on finishing and hiding the raw edges of the ends of the binding.

CONTINUOUS BIAS BINDING

A continuous bias binding involves using a square sliced in half diagonally and then sewing the triangles together so that you continuously cut marked strips to make continuous bias binding. The same instructions can be used to cut bias for piping. Cut the fabric for the bias binding or piping so it is a square. For example, if yardage is ½ yard, cut an 18″ × 18″ square. Cut the square in half diagonally, creating 2 triangles.

Sew these triangles together as shown, using a ¼″ seam allowance. Press the seam open.

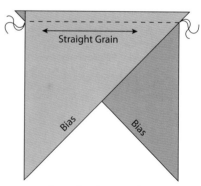

Straight Grain

Bias   Bias

Sew triangles together.

Using a ruler, mark the parallelogram created by the 2 triangles with lines spaced the width you need to cut your bias. Cut about 5″ along the first line.

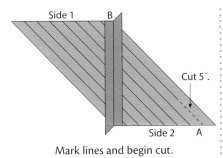

Side 1   B

Cut 5˝.

Side 2   A

Mark lines and begin cut.

Join Side 1 and Side 2 to form a tube. The raw edge at Line A will align with the raw edge at B. This will allow the first line to be offset by 1 strip width. Pin the raw edges right sides together, making sure that the lines match. Sew with a ¼˝ seam allowance. Press the seam open. Cut along the drawn lines, creating a continuous strip.

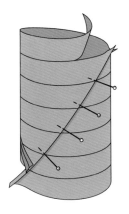

Press the entire strip in half length-wise, with wrong sides together. Place the binding on the quilt as described in Double-Fold Straight Grain Binding (page 59).

See Finishing the Binding Ends (below) for tips on finishing and hiding the raw edges of the ends of the binding.

FINISHING THE BINDING ENDS

Method 1

After stitching around the quilt, fold under the beginning tail of the binding strip ¼˝ so that the raw edge will be inside the binding after it is turned to the backside of the quilt. Place the end tail of the binding strip over the beginning folded end. Continue to attach the binding and stitch slightly beyond the starting stitches. Trim the excess binding. Fold the binding over the raw edges to the quilt back and hand stitch, mitering the corners.

Method 2

See the blog entry at ctpubblog.com > search "invisible seam" > scroll down to "Quilting Tips: Completing a binding with an invisible seam."

Fold the ending tail of the binding back on itself where it meets the beginning binding tail. From the fold, measure and mark the cut width of your binding strip. Cut the ending

binding tail to this measurement. For example, if your binding is cut 2½" wide, measure from the fold on the ending tail of the binding 2½" and cut the binding tail to this length.

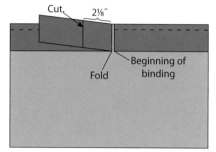

Cut binding tail.

Open both tails. Place 1 tail on top of the other tail at right angles, right sides together. Mark a diagonal line from corner to corner and stitch on the line. Check that you've done it correctly and that the binding fits the quilt. Then trim the seam allowance to ¼". Press open.

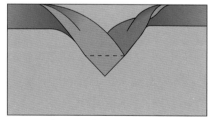

Stitch ends of binding diagonally.

Refold the binding and stitch this binding section in place on the quilt. Fold the binding over the raw edges to the quilt back and hand stitch.

about the author

Photo by Sean Cier

Emily Cier, creator of Carolina Patchworks, has had a lifelong love of fine art and art history and has a background in graphic design. These passions finally found a common ground in quilting, which she quickly discovered to be a wonderful and timeless creative outlet, as well as one filled with a rich history. It also keeps her quite toasty on a cold day and gives her an excuse to visit the local quilt shop on a daily basis. How can you beat that?

Emily lives with her husband and two beautiful children (who are showing their own penchant for creativity).

Visit her website at www.carolinapatchworks.com.

resources

Rotary Circle Cutter (CMP-3)

> OLFA - North America Division
> www.olfa.com
> 5500 N. Pearl Street, Suite 400
> Rosemont, IL 60018

Quilter's Freezer Paper Sheets
Carol Doak's Foundation Paper
fast2cut® Half- & Quarter-Diamond Ruler Set

> C&T Publishing, Inc.
> www.ctpub.com

Great Titles *from* C&T PUBLISHING

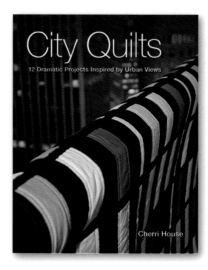

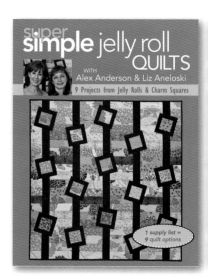

Available at your local retailer or **www.ctpub.com** *or* **800-284-1114**

For a list of other fine books from C&T Publishing, ask for a free catalog:

C&T PUBLISHING, INC.
P.O. Box 1456
Lafayette, CA 94549
800-284-1114

Email: ctinfo@ctpub.com
Website: www.ctpub.com

C&T Publishing's professional photography services are now available to the public. Visit us at www.ctmediaservices.com.

Tips and Techniques can be found at www.ctpub.com > Consumer Resources > Quiltmaking Basics: Tips & Techniques for Quiltmaking & More

For quilting supplies:

COTTON PATCH
1025 Brown Ave.
Lafayette, CA 94549
Store: 925-284-1177
Mail order: 925-283-7883

Email: CottonPa@aol.com
Website: www.quiltusa.com

Note: Fabrics used in the quilts shown may not be currently available, as fabric manufacturers keep most fabrics in print for only a short time.